Hilarious
HOLIDAY
Humor

Richard Lederer & Stan Kegel
International Punsters of the Year

Illustrations by Jim McLean

Marion Street Press
Portland, Oregon

To Caroline McCullagh, who makes my books better
—*Richard Lederer*

To my many patients who over the years have tried
to stump me with their riddles and, to their joy,
have frequently succeeded
—*Stan Kegel*

Published by Marion Street Press
4207 SE Woodstock Blvd # 168
Portland, OR 97206-6267
USA
http://www.marionstreetpress.com

Orders and review copies: (800) 888-4741

Printed in the United States of America

ISBN 9781936863518

Library of Congress Cataloging-in-Publication Data pending

Contents

New Year's Eve / New Year's Day 4

Groundhog Day 7

Valentine's Day... 9

Presidents' Day...13

St. Patrick's Day 16

April Fools' Day 19

Passover 26

Easter 30

Cinco de Mayo 35

Independence Day.. 37

Labor Day 41

Columbus Day... 44

Halloween 46

Thanksgiving 70

Chanukah 78

Christmas Eve / Christmas Day 83

New Year's Eve /
New Year's Day

*C*alendars were first made so that people could predict recurring events, such as planting and harvest times. In 45 B.C., Julius Caesar ordered that the new year be celebrated on January first to honor Janus, the god of beginnings and gatekeeper of heaven and earth. Janus was a double-faced god who looked forward into the new year and backward to the old. The name Janus gave us the word *January*.

The passing of one year into the beginning of another is marked around the world by New Year's Eve customs ranging from high-spirited parties to solemn prayer and thought. The biggest and most famous New Year's party takes place in New York City. Millions of people around the world watch the ginormous Waterford Crystal Ball drop over Times Square.

"Auld Lang Syne," written by the Scottish poet Robert Burns, is the song most identified with New Year's celebrations. We all know "Auld Lang Syne," even though few of us really know what it means, which happens to be "old long since." The song was first popularized in 1929 by Guy Lombardo and his Royal Canadians orchestra.

On January 1, we make New Year's resolutions, vowing to better ourselves in the coming year. Many of these resolutions are forgotten as soon as they're made, but the sentiment remains noble. Taking a few moments to reflect on our shortcomings and optimistically plan to overcome them is better than making no attempt at all. And sometimes, when we are ready for change, those resolutions do stick—some for a few months, some for a year, and some for a lifetime.

Happy New Year. It's nice to have You Near! Here are the ways people in various jobs wish one another the start of the year:

> *from a lumberjack:* "Choppy New Year!"
> *a hip hop artist:* "Rappy New Year!"
> *a maple syrup seller:* "Sappy New Year!"
> *a cartographer:* "Mappy New Year!"
> *a laser gunner:* "Zappy New Year!"
> *a detective:* "Happy Clue Year!"
> *a cobbler:* "Happy Shoe Year!"
> *a sea captain:* "Happy Crew Year!"
> *a lawyer:* "Happy Sue Year!"
> *a surfer:* "Happy Dude Year!"
> *a priest:* "Happy Pew Year!"
> *a job counselor:* "Happy New Career!"
> *a mechanic:* "Happy Lube Gear!"

And here are the ways some animals would say it:

> *from a puppy:* "Yappy, Lappy New Year!"
> *a kitten:* "Happy Mew Year!"
> *a turtle:* "Snappy New Year!"
> *a skunk:* "Happy Eeeeewww Year!"
> *a duck:* "Quacky New Year!"

cattle: "Happy Moo Steer!"
a large water beast: "Hippo New Year!"
an antelope: "Happy Gnu Deer!"
a kangaroo, a frog, a toad, and a bunny: "Hoppy New Year!"

Groundhog Day

Since 1886, each February 2 we celebrate Groundhog Day. The official groundhog is named Punxsutawney Phil because he lives in Punxsutawney, Pennsylvania. His full title is "Punxsutawney Phil, Seer of Seers, Sage of Sages, Prognosticator of Prognosticators, and Weather Prophet Extraordinary."

The large rodent comes out of his burrow at Gobbler's Knob to predict the weather for the rest of season. Thousands of followers from all over the world look on. These fans use the occasion to relieve cabin fever. And they figure that Phil's prediction is as reliable as that of the National Weather Service.

As the story goes, if February 2 is bright and clear and Punxsutawney Phil sees his shadow, we can expect six more weeks of winter weather. If the day is overcast and Phil doesn't see his shadow, there will be an early spring. The idea for Groundhog Day began with Pennsylvania's earliest settlers. It stemmed from a combination of religious beliefs (Candlemas Day) and beliefs about hibernating animals:

> *If Candlemas be fair and bright,*
> *Come, Winter, have another flight.*
> *If Candlemas brings clouds and rain,*
> *Go Winter, and come not again.*

A Pig Deal

Pig farmers have it rough. Most Americans prefer beef to pork, and hamburger is an American favorite but contains no ham. In addition, we eat more poultry, fish, and vegetables, while the sale of pork, ham, and bacon have remained unchanged.

Because of this, The National Piggy Association hired a big Madison Avenue advertising firm to boost sales of pork. They put ads in magazines, television, and radio urging people to eat pork patties.

The campaign got an extra boost when Congress decided to make the second of February the day when every family would be urged to eat pork sausage. That day would be celebrated nationally as Ground Hog Day.

At a State Fair a big prize was awarded to the owners of the pig that weighed the most. The contest was called Round Hog Day.

What's green, has four legs, and jumps out of its hole every February 2?

A groundfrog.

What do you get if you cross a groundhog with a puppy?

A grounddog.

Did you hear about the student who saw her shadow on Groundhog Day and predicted six more weeks of detentions?

What do you call Punxsutawney Phil's laundry?

Hogwash.

Valentine's Day

Valentine's Day, a day of love and romance, probably originated from the ancient Roman feast of Lupercalia. On the eve of that festival, the names of Roman girls were written on slips of paper and placed into jars. Each young man drew a slip, and the girl whose name he chose became his sweetheart for the year.

Legend has it that the holiday was named after Valentine, a Christian priest in third-century Rome when Christianity was a new religion. The Emperor Claudius II forbade Roman soldiers to marry, believing that, as married men, his soldiers would prefer to stay home with their families rather than fight his wars.

Valentine defied the Emperor's rule and secretly married young couples. He was eventually arrested, imprisoned, and put to death on February 14, 269, the eve of Lupercalia. After his death, Valentine was made a saint. As Rome became more Christian, the Feast of the Lupercal became St. Valentine's Day, observed each February 14.

Modern Valentine's Day symbols include the heart shape, doves, and the figure of the winged Cupid. The tradition of sending Valentine's cards did not become widespread in the United States until the 1850s, when Esther A. Howland began mass-producing them. Since then, millions of Valentine's Day greetings cards have been exchanged, electronically and otherwise. Scads of bouquets of flowers and boxes of chocolates are given, and couples often enjoy a romantic dinner together at home or in a restaurant.

Why do valentines have hearts on them?
Because kidneys would look pretty gross.

What do you call a dumb little boy with wings and a bow and arrow?
A stupid cupid.

What does a man who loves his car do on February 14?
He gives it a valenshine.

What does a little person give his wife for Valentine's Day?
A valentiny card.

What did the caveman give his wife on Valentine's Day?
Uggs and kisses.

What did the French chef give his wife for Valentine's Day?
A hug and a quiche.

What did Frankenstein say to his ghoul friend?

"Be my valenstein!"

What did the painter say to her boyfriend?

"I love you with all my art!"

What did the paper clip say to the magnet on Valentine's Day?

"I find you very attractive."

What did one pickle say to the other on Valentine's Day?

"You mean a great dill to me."

What did one light bulb say to the other on Valentine's Day?

"I love you a whole watt! You're so bright, and you turn me on!"

What did the valentine card say to the stamp?

"I'm stuck on you. Now you stick with me and we'll go places!"

And what do animals say to each other on Valentine's Day?:

a cat: "You're a purrr-fect mate for me!"

a pig: "Happy Valenswine's Day. I give you many hogs and kisses!"

a skunk: "I'm very scent-imental about you!"

a bat: "You're fun to hang around with."

an elephant: "I love you a ton!"

a sheep: "I love ewe in a wild and woolly way!"

a pigeon: "I dove coo, tweetheart!"

a dog: "I love you drool-ly!"

a squirrel: "I'm bright-eyed and bushy-tailed and nuts about you!"

a snake: "Give me a little bug and a hiss!"

an octopus: "I wanna hold your hand, hand, hand, hand, hand, hand, hand, hand!"

a centipede: "I love you so much that I'd wait on you hand and foot, foot, foot, foot, foot, foot, foot, foot, foot, foot . . . !"

Presidents' Day

*P*residents' Day is a federal holiday on the third Monday of February. The original celebration was in honor of George Washington, whose actual birthday was February 22. Abraham Lincoln, who was born February 12, was added to the mix. In the late 1980s, Presidents' Day became the official name of the holiday, which honors the men who have held the most powerful office in the world.

How do we know that anyone can become president of the United States?

Jefferson did it. Nixon did it. And Truman did it. So any Tom, Dick, and Harry can be president!

What would you get if you crossed George Washington with cattle feed?

The Fodder of Our Country.

What would you get if you crossed our first president with a wood sculptor?

George Washington Carver.

What would you get if you crossed George Washington's home with nasty rodents?

Mount Vermin.

Having bad teeth, what did our first president wear in his mouth?

The George Washington Bridge.

Where did George Washington buy his hatchet?

At the chopping mall.

What did George Washington say as he stood on the boat crossing the Delaware?

"Next time I'm going to reserve a seat."

If George Washington were alive today, why couldn't he throw a silver dollar across the Potomac?

Because a dollar doesn't go as far as it used to.

Why is Abraham Lincoln our least guilty president?

Because he's in a cent.

What does an owl in the daytime have in common with our 16th president?

They're both A-blinkin'.

What was General Ulysses Grant's favorite tree?

The infant-tree.

If Theodore Roosevelt were alive today, what would he be famous for?

Old age.

What was Franklin D. Roosevelt's favorite fish?

The Nude Eel.

In history books, where can you find Bill Clinton?

Between two Bushes.

Name five presidents of the United States who are not buried in the United States.

All the ones who are still alive.

St. Patrick's Day

S t. Patrick is the patron saint of Ireland. Legend has it that he drove the snakes out of Ireland, although in fact snakes were never there. The legend may be referring to Patrick's expelling the Druidic religion and bringing Christianity to the Emerald Isle. Patrick died on March 17, A.D. 460, and the Catholic Church made that his saint's day. As a result, March 17 is the date of St. Patrick's Day each year.

In the United States, more than 30 million people claim at least some Irish heritage, and on March 17 each year, everybody becomes Irish. Many cities host annual St. Patrick's Day parades in which Irish pride is on display.

Emblems of St. Patrick's Day include leprechauns, shamrocks, and anything green, from clothing to food. Restaurants and bars serve corned beef and cabbage, washed down with green beer. The city of Chicago even adds a temporary dye to the Chicago River to turn it green for a day.

Knock, knock.

Who's there?

Irish.

Irish who?

Irish you a happy St. Patrick's Day.

Why did St. Patrick drive the snakes out of Ireland?

Because it was too far for them to crawl and he couldn't afford plane fare.

Why do people wear shamrocks on St. Patrick's Day?

Because real rocks are too heavy.

First Woman: "I married an Irishman on St. Patrick's Day."

Second Woman: "Oh, really?"

First Woman: "No, O'Reilly."

What's Irish and sits out on your lawn all summer?

Paddy O'Furniture.

Did you hear about the man who wanted to sound Irish?

He decided to go for brogue.

What's the secret to cooking a tasty Irish stew?
Add a pinch of Gaelic.

Why can't you borrow money from a leprechaun?
Because they're always a little short.

What do you call a leprechaun who works at a diner?
A short order cook.

Where would you find a leprechaun in a baseball game?
Playing shortstop in the Little League.

What did the leprechaun say to the elf?
"How's the weather up there?"

What's little and green and stuck in your car's front bumper?
A leprechaun who didn't look both ways.

What are Irish men and women doing when they read the jokes in this book?
They're Dublin over with laughter.

April Fools' Day

*U*nlike most holidays, no one knows the origin of April Fools' Day. We do know that before the Gregorian calendar became standard in Europe, the New Year was celebrated from March 22 until April 1. We also know April Fools' Day became widely celebrated in England in the 1800s.

April Fools' Day, sometimes called All Fools' Day, is a time to play pranks on others. These tricks can be verbal, as in the examples below, or they can be physical. Plastic wrap on the toilet seat, alarm clocks set back an hour, and the classic "kick me" sign affixed to a friend's back are a few popular April Fools' Day pranks.

Have a very happy April Fools' Day, but don't forget to watch your back!

Read the following nursery rhyme and then answer the question posed in the last line:

> As I was going to St. Ives,
> I met a man with seven wives.
> Every wife had seven sacks.
> Every sack had seven cats.
> Every cat had seven kits.
> Kits, cats, sacks, wives—
> How many were going to St. Ives?

The answer to the question is one. While the man and his wives and their sacks, cats, and kits were going from St. Ives, only the speaker—the *I* in the rhyme—was going to St. Ives.

If you madly multiplied 7 times 7 times 7 times 7 and added one for the man, you were the victim of a language trap. Language traps test your ability to read or listen carefully and to avoid being fooled by misinformation. If you think as you consider the 32 classic language traps in this game, you can avoid being called an April fool. Answers immediately follow the questions.

1. Name three consecutive days without using the words Wednesday, Friday, or Sunday.

2. Which is correct: (a) 9 and 7 *is* 15 or (b) 9 and 7 *are* 15?

3. How many three-cent stamps are there in a dozen?

4. Pronounce out loud the words formed by each of the following letter series: B-O-A-S-T, C-O-A-S-T, R-O-A-S-T. Now, what do you put in a toaster?

5. Pronounce out loud the words formed by each of the following letter series: B-I-L-K, S-I-L-K. Now, what do cows drink?

6. If a red house is made from red bricks and a blue house is made from blue bricks, what is a greenhouse made of?

7. A doctor is about to operate on a little boy. "This child is my son!" exclaims the doctor. The doctor is correct, yet the doctor is not the boy's father. What is going on?

8. If a peacock and a half lays an egg and a half in a day and a half, how many eggs will three peacocks lay in three days?

9. Do they have a fourth of July in England?

10. Two men play five games of checkers, and each wins the same number of games. There are no draws. How can this be?

11. A farmer had 17 sheep. All but nine died. How many were left alive?

12. If a bus leaves from Boston to New York City an hour before another bus leaves from New York City to Boston, which bus will be closer to Boston when the two pass each other?

13. A rope ladder is hanging over the side of a ship. The ladder is 12 feet long, and the rungs are one foot apart, with the lowest rung resting on the surface of the water. The water is rising at a rate of one foot an hour. How long will it take before the first three rungs are underwater?

14. What was the highest mountain on earth before Mount Everest was discovered?

15. What were Alexander Graham Bell's first words?

16. If two is company and three is a crowd, what are four and five?

17. How many times can you subtract 5 from 25?

18. How much dirt is there in a hole three feet by three feet by three feet?

19. In the United States is it legal for a man to marry his widow's sister?

20. Pronounce out loud the word formed by each of the following letter series: M-A-C-D-O-N-A-L-D, M-A-C-B-E-T-H, M-A-C-H-I-N-E-R-Y.

21. One child playing on a beach has made four-and-a-half sand piles. Another child has made two-and-a-half sand piles. They decide to put all their sand piles together. How many sand piles do they now have?

22. If an airplane crashes on the Maine-New Hampshire border, in which state would the survivors be buried?

23. I have in my hand two U.S. coins that total 30 cents. One is not a nickel. What are the two coins?

24. How many mistakes can you find in this sentence?: "Their are five mistaiks in this sentance."

25. Read the following sentence slowly and only once, counting the number of *F*'s:

    FINISHED FILES ARE THE RESULT
    OF YEARS OF SCIENTIFIC STUDY

    How many *F*'s did you find?

26. A dog is tied to a 20-foot leash yet is able to run to a bone lying 50 feet away. The leash does not stretch or break in any way. How is this possible?

27. Mary and Jane were born on the same day of the same year to the same father and mother. They look almost exactly alike, yet they are not twins. How can this be?

28. Which is correct: "The capitol of Pennsylvania is Philadelphia" or "The capital of Pennsylvania is Philadelphia"?

29. If you drop a rock, would it fall more rapidly through water at 40 degrees Fahrenheit or 20 degrees Fahrenheit?

30. Attempting to get out of a well that is 30 feet deep, a frog, starting at the bottom, hops up three feet and falls back two with each attempt. How many tries will it take the frog to reach the top of the well?

31. My name is Stan, and I have five sisters. Each of my sisters has one brother. How many children did my parents have?

32. The number of people in a movie theater doubles every five minutes. After an hour, the theater is full. When was the theater half full?

33. You are the engineer on a train going from Chicago to New York. The train leaves Chicago with a hundred passengers, stops in Detroit to pick up ten and discharge five, stops in Cleveland to pick up five and discharge ten, stops in Buffalo to pick up ten and discharge five, and then proceeds to New York.

How old is the engineer?

Answers

1. Yesterday, today, and tomorrow. 2. The sum of 9 and 7 is 16. 3. twelve 4. bread 5. water

6. glass 7. The doctor is the boy's mother. 8. None. Peacocks don't lay eggs; peahens do. 9. Of course. July 4th occurs between July 3rd and July 5th. 10. Each man was playing a different opponent.

11. Nine 12. When the two buses are passing each other, both will be the same distance from Boston. 13. The rungs will never be underwater because the ship rises with the tide. 14. Mount Everest 15. No one knows for sure, but probably "mama" and "dada."

16. Nine 17. Once. After that, the number is 20. 18. There is no dirt in a hole. 19. If a man has a widow, he is likely to be quite dead. 20. The last word is pronounced *masheenery*, not *MacHinery*.

21. One 22. Survivors aren't buried anywhere. 23. One is not a nickel; it's a quarter. The other coin is a nickel. 24. Four. Because there are only three errors in the sentence, the word *five* becomes the fourth mistake. 25. Five. Most people get only three.

26. Nobody said that the other end of the leash was tied to anything. 27. They are two members of a set of triplets. 28. The capital of Pennsylvania is Harrisburg. 29. Forty degrees. A rock can't fall through ice. 30. Twenty-eight tries. After the twenty-seventh, the frog will reach the top with its next hop of three feet.

31. Six—five sisters and one brother (the speaker) 32. After 55 minutes 33. Because you are the engineer, the age of the engineer is your age.

Passover

*P*assover is a Jewish festival commemorating the exodus ("escape") of Israelite slaves from Egypt. The holiday is named to remember God's "passing over" the houses of the Jewish people during the plague that killed Egyptian firstborn sons.

The Passover Seder includes a meal during which worshipers read from the Haggadah and discuss the history and reasons for celebrating the holiday. The first of two Seders starts on the fifteenth day of Nissan, which is the first month of the Hebrew calendar. The celebrants eat bitter herbs and matzo, which is unleavened ("not risen") bread. These foods recall the bitter years of slavery and the fact that the escaping Hebrews did not have enough time to leaven their bread.

Because the Jews were forced to leave ancient Egypt before their bread could rise, leavened products are not to be consumed during Passover. A type of spring cleaning, during which all traces of leavened grain products are thoroughly eliminated, takes place in the 30 days prior to the start of Passover. This practice is symbolic of removing "puffiness" (arrogance) from the soul.

A little boy returned home from Hebrew school and his father asked, "What did you learn today?"

"The rabbi told us how Moses led the children of Israel out of Egypt."

"How?"

The boy explained, "Moses was a big strong man and he beat Pharaoh up. Then while he was down, he got all the people together and ran toward the sea. When he got there, he had the Corps of Engineers build a huge pontoon bridge. Once they got on the other side, they blew up the bridge while the Egyptians were trying to cross."

The father was shocked. "Is that what the rabbi taught you?"

The boy replied, "No. But you'd never believe the story he did tell us!"

A Jewish man took his Passover lunch to eat outside in the park. He sat down on a bench and began eating. Since Jews do not eat leavened bread during the eight-day holiday, he was eating matzo, a flat crunchy unleavened bread that has dozens of ridges and little holes.

A short while later, a blind man came by and sat down next to him. Feeling neighborly, the Jewish man passed a sheet of matzo to the blind man.

The blind man handled the matzo for a few minutes, looked puzzled, and finally asked, "Who wrote this stuff?"

Every Passover at the Seder table, every Jewish child will be retold the story of Moses and the Pharaoh and how God sent boils, locusts, hail, and the other plagues upon the Egyptians. In spite of God's actions, Pharaoh refused to let the Jews go, until a tenth plague, the death of the first-born male children, was inflicted on every Egyptian home. Only after this did Pharaoh give up and let the Jews leave Egypt to begin their journey to the promised land.

Why did Pharaoh again and again refuse to let the Jewish people go?

Because Pharaoh lived in a state of De Nile.

And why did Moses lead the Israelites all over the place for 40 years before they finally got to the Promised Land?

He didn't stop to ask for directions.

There's No Seder Like Our Seder
(sung to the tune of
"There's No Business Like Show Business")

There's no Seder like our Seder,
There's no Seder I know.
Everything about it is halachic,
Nothing that the Torah won't allow.
Listen how we read the whole Haggadah.
It's all in Hebrew, 'cause we know how.

There's no Seder like our Seder.
There's no Seder I know.
Moses took the people out into the heat.
They baked the matzo while on their feet.
Now isn't that a story that just can't be beat?
Let's go on with the show! Let's go on with the show!

Easter

*E*aster honors the resurrection of Jesus Christ on the third day after his crucifixion. Easter was the earliest feast day decreed by the ancient Christian Church. Many Christians consider Easter to be the most important holiday in their faith.

Like its Jewish predecessor, Passover, Easter is a movable feast, based on the lunar calendar rather than occurring on the same Sunday every year. This holiday can fall as early as March 22 and as late as April 25.

Among the traditions associated with Easter is the Easter Hare, or, in America, the Easter Bunny, who brings baskets of candies and colored eggs during the night. In the 1700s, German settlers brought with them the idea of the Easter Bunny, a symbol of new life during the spring season.

Children believed that if they were good, the Easter Bunny would lay a nest of colorful eggs.

Easter Sunday ends the long fast of Lent. Women don stylish Easter bonnets, and families display and consume food, such as Easter candy, Easter breads, hot cross buns, and Easter eggs. Often families have Easter egg hunts for the youngest children. Hard-boiled eggs are brightly decorated and then hidden for boys and girls to uncover.

A man was happily driving along the highway, when he saw the Easter Bunny hopping across the middle of the road. He swerved to avoid hitting the Bunny, but unfortunately the rabbit hopped in front of his car. The basket of eggs went flying all over the place. Candy, too.

The driver pulled over to the side of the road and got out to see what had become of the bunny carrying the basket. Much to his dismay, the colorful bunny was dead. The driver felt guilty and began to cry.

A woman driving down the same highway saw the man crying on the side of the road and pulled over. She told the man not to worry. She knew exactly what to do. She went to her car trunk, and pulled out a spray can. She walked over to the limp, dead Bunny, and sprayed the entire contents of the can onto the little furry animal.

Miraculously the Easter Bunny came to back life, jumped up, picked up the spilled eggs and candy, waved its paw at the two humans, and hopped on down the road. Fifty yards away the Easter Bunny stopped, turned around, waved, and hopped on down the road another 50 yards, turned, waved, hopped another 50 yards, and waved again!

The man was astonished. He asked the woman, "What was it that you sprayed on the Easter Bunny?"

The woman turned the can around so that the man could read the label. It said: "Hare spray: Restores life to dead hare. Adds permanent wave."

How is the Easter Bunny like LeBron James?
They're both famous for stuffing baskets.

What do Easter Bunny helpers get for making a basket?
Two points, just like anyone else.

What is the Easter Bunny's favorite state capital?
Albunny, New York.

What would you get if you crossed the Easter Bunny with a famous French general?
Napoleon Bunnyparte.

What's big and purple and hugs your Easter basket?
The Easter Barney.

What do you call an egg-laden rabbit who jumps off bridges?
The Easter Bungee.

How does the Easter Bunny paint all of those eggs?
He hires Santa's elves during the off-season.

How should you send a letter to the Easter Bunny?
By hare mail.

How do you make a rabbit stew?
Make it wait for three hours.

What has big ears, brings Easter treats, and goes hippity-BOOM hippity-BOOM?
The Easter Elephant.

Why shouldn't you tell an Easter egg a good joke?
It might crack up.

What do you call a line of Easter bunnies walking backwards?
A receding hareline.

What do you call rabbits that marched in a long, sweltering Easter parade?

Hot cross bunnies.

What do you call a rabbit with fleas?

Bugs Bunny.

Why do we paint Easter eggs?

Because it's easier than trying to wallpaper them.

What did the rabbit say to the carrot?

"It's been nice gnawing you."

Why did the magician have to cancel her Easter show?

She'd just washed her hare and couldn't do a thing with it.

How does the Easter Bunny make gold soup?

He begins with 24 carrots.

What would you get if you crossed the Easter Bunny with Chinese food?

Hop suey.

What is the Easter Bunny's favorite dance style?

Hip-hop.

Who is the Easter Bunny's favorite movie actor?

Rabbit De Niro.

Boy 1: "How did you get that bruise on your arm?"
Boy 2: "I ate some Easter candy."
Boy 1: "Eating Easter candy won't give you a bruise."
Boy 2: "It will if it's your big brother's candy!"

Cinco de Mayo

Cinco de Mayo is a Mexican holiday remembering the defeat of the French army at the Battle of Puebla on May 5, 1862. Today, Puebla's Cinco de Mayo ("5th of May") celebration is among the largest and most festive in the world.

The recognition of Cinco de Mayo history quickly spread from Mexico to the United States, where it is primarily a celebration of the culture of America's southern neighbor. Cinco de Mayo parties include plenty of specially prepared Mexican food—a good guacamole, tacos, enchiladas, burritos, and plenty of Latin spices. The holiday is usually an outdoor affair, and the pleasant spring weather is perfect for firing up the grill and cooking some sizzling barbecue, Mexican style.

Cinco de Mayo parties are often adorned with brightly colored streamers and Mexican flags flapping in the wind. No Cinco de Mayo bash is complete without a piñata, a decorated vessel, often made of papier-mâché, filled with candy, fruit, and gifts. Piñatas are hung up for blindfolded people, usually children, to break open with sticks—the best way to punctuate a Cinco de Mayo celebration.

In the early 1900s, Hellman's Mayonnaise was made in England. In 1912, the company asked the Titanic to deliver 12,000 jars of the condiment to Vera Cruz, Mexico, which was to be the next port of call for the great ship after its stop in New York.

This would have been the largest single shipment of mayonnaise ever delivered to Mexico. But as we know, the great ship did not make it to New York. It struck an iceberg and sank, and the cargo was forever lost.

The people of Mexico, who were crazy about mayonnaise and were eagerly awaiting its delivery, were saddened by the loss. Their sadness was so great that they declared a National Day of Mourning, which they still observe to this day—Sinko de Mayo.

Independence Day

*O*ne of the most festive holidays of the summer is Independence Day—the Fourth of July. On that day, we celebrate the freedom of the colonies that broke away from the authority that had been imposed on them by England and formed the United States of America. On the Fourth of July, we remember the signing of the Declaration of Independence, which expressed the desires of the new American citizens and proclaimed their belief in three basic rights—life, liberty, and the pursuit of happiness.

So this summer, halfway between Memorial Day and Labor Day, as you're getting out your festive red, white, and blue decorations or eating a hot dog at a barbecue or cheering at a baseball game or gawking at spectacular fireworks, stop for a moment and think about those who fought in the Revolutionary War. Many endured hardships and died so that we could live in the freedom that we enjoy today. Without their bravery and will to stand up to England and fight for their right to be free, our United States of America would be a much different place.

Knock, knock
Who's there?
Llama
Llama who?
Llama Yankee Doodle Dandy

Each July I say, "May the Fourth be with you!"

What did a patriot put on his dry skin?
Revo-lotion.

What did the big firework say to the little firework?
My pop is bigger than your pop.

Where was the Declaration of Independence signed?
On the bottom.

What did King George think of the American colonists?
He thought they were revolting.

The Fourth of July weekend was coming up, and the nursery school teacher talked to her class about patriotism. "We live in a great country," she said. "One of the things we should be happy about is that, in this country, we are all free."

One little boy came walking up to her from the back of the room. He stood with his hands on his hips and said, "I'm not free. I'm four."

Teacher: "The Declaration of Independence was written in Philadelphia. True or false?"

Student: "False! It was written in ink!"

What ghost haunted King George III?
> *The spirit of '76.*

Did you hear about the cartoonist in the Continental Army?
> *He was a Yankee doodler.*

Did you hear the one about the Liberty Bell?
> *Yeah, it cracked me up.*

Why did the duck say, "Bang!"?
> *Because he was a firequacker!*

What dance was very popular in 1776?
> *The Indepen-dance.*

What happened as a result of the Stamp Act?
> *The Americans licked the British.*

Why did Paul Revere ride his horse from Boston to Lexington?
> *Because the horse was too heavy to carry.*

What would you get if you crossed a patriot with a small curly-haired dog?
> *A Yankee Poodle.*

What's red, white, blue, and yellow?
> *The Star-Spangled Banana.*

How is a flag like Santa Claus?

They both hang out at the pole.

What has stars and stripes?

A movie about tigers, skunks, and zebras.

What do you call the tigers, skunks, and zebras that hang out with Tarzan?

The Tarzan stripes.

Betsy Ross asked a group of colonists for their opinions of the flag that she had made. It was the first flag poll.

What did one flag say to the other flag?

Nothing. It just waved.

Labor Day

*L*abor Day was first celebrated in New York City in 1882, when the Central Labor Union held its first parade to show the spirit of its trade and labor groups. The show of solidarity went national in 1885, after a vote by the body that became the American Federation of Labor. Now observed in every American state, Labor Day also signals with the unofficial end of the summer season.

In North America, it is celebrated on the first Monday in September. Many cities offer planned events in local parks and fairgrounds, and many families arrange picnics. These days, Labor Day is largely a time for family togetherness and relaxation. Cookouts, barbecues, and leisure activities such as boating, fishing, camping, and picnicking are popular ways to spend the Labor Day weekend as people seek to enjoy the warm weather while it lasts and take best advantage of the summer sunshine before autumn sets in.

In honor of Labor Day, I share with you my personal workplace history:

My first job was in an orange juice factory, but I couldn't concentrate on the same old boring rind, so I got canned.

Then I worked in the woods as a lumberjack, but I just couldn't hack it, so they gave me the axe.

After that, I tried working in a donut shop, but I soon got tired of the hole business.

I manufactured calendars, but my days were numbered.

I tried to be a tailor, but I just wasn't suited for it. Mainly because it was a sew-sew job, de-pleating and de-pressing.

I took a job as an upholsterer, but I never recovered.

Next I tried working in a car muffler factory, but that was exhausting.

I took a job as an elevator operator. The job had its ups and downs, and I got the shaft.

I wanted to be a barber, but I just couldn't cut it.

I sold origami, but the business folded.

I studied a long time to become a doctor, but I didn't have enough patients for the job.

I took a job at UPS, but I couldn't express myself.

I next worked in a shoe factory, but I just didn't fit in. They thought I was a loafer, and I got the boot.

I became a Velcro and Crazy Glue salesman, but couldn't stick with it.

I was a professional fisherman, but I couldn't live on my net income.

I became a baker, but it wasn't a cakewalk, and I couldn't make enough dough.

I thought about being a historian, but I couldn't see a future in it.

I was a masseur for a while, but I rubbed people the wrong way.

I became a Hawaiian garland maker, but I got leid off.

I tried being a fireman, but I suffered burnout.

I became a banker, but I lacked interest and maturity and finally withdrew from the job.

I managed to get a good job working for a pool maintenance company, but the work was just too draining.

I got a job at a zoo feeding giraffes, but I was fired because I wasn't up to it.

Then I became a personal trainer in a gym, but they said I wasn't fit for the job.

Next I was an electrician, but I found the work shocking and revolting, so they discharged me.

I became a tennis pro, but it wasn't my racket. I was too high strung.

I tried being a teacher, but I soon lost my principal, my faculties, and my class.

I turned to farming, but I wasn't outstanding in my field.

Then I was a pilot, but tended to wing it, and I didn't have the right altitude.

I worked at Starbucks, but I had to quit because it was always the same old grind.

So I've retired, and I find I'm a perfect fit for this job!

Columbus Day

*C*hristopher Columbus (1451–1506) is generally given credit for discovering America. In school most of us learned this ditty:

> *In fourteen hundred ninety two,*
> *Columbus sailed the ocean blue.*

And he did. On his first voyage, he sighted the Bahamas and made land on Hispaniola (now Haiti and the Dominican Republic).

Columbus Day is a holiday that honors the famous explorer's arrival, on October 12, 1492, in the New World. The holiday was first officially celebrated across the United States in 1937.

Columbus Day boat races are a common way the holiday is celebrated in many parts of the United States. Most schools close for Columbus Day, as do government offices and banks, while most businesses remain open.

What bus was able to get to America by sea?

Columbus.

How do we know that Columbus was the best deal-maker in history?

> *He left not knowing where he was going. When he got there, he didn't know where he was. When he returned, he didn't know where he'd been. And he did it all on borrowed money.*

How did King Ferdinand and Queen Isabella pay for Columbus's voyages?

With their Discover card.

What do the Nina, the Pinta, and the Santa Maria have in common with a department store?

They're all driven by sails.

How do we know that Columbus's ships got the best gas mileage in history?

They got three thousand miles per galleon.

Halloween

*F*alling on October 31, Halloween is the year's spookiest holiday. On that day we carve faces in pumpkins, dress in horrible costumes, and go out trick-or-treating.

The traditions associated with modern-day Halloween find their roots in ancient Ireland, in the fifth century B.C. October 31 signaled the end of the Celtic year and the beginning of winter. On this day, the Celts commemorate Samhain (pronounced "Sow-wen"), a festival that celebrates the final harvest and the food stored for the winter ahead.

The presence of witches, ghosts, and cats in Halloween traditions originates with the Druids. The Druids were an order of priests in ancient Gaul and Britain who believed that ghosts, spirits, fairies, witches, and elves came out on All Hallows' Eve to harm people. They thought that cats had once been people but were changed as punishment for their evil deeds.

Over the centuries, the holiday evolved from its pagan Irish origins. In the seventh century A.D., Pope Boniface IV introduced All Saints' Day, to replace the pagan festivals honoring the dead. The holiday was also known as All Hallows' Day, and the preceding night was named All Hallows' Eve, which has become shortened to "Halloween."

In Ireland grew up the custom of carving out the insides of turnips and lighting them with embers to represent the souls of the dead. In the 1840s, Irish immigrants fleeing their country's potato famine brought the tradition to America. They replaced turnips with the more abundant pumpkins. From pumpkins they created jack-o'-lanterns, and the practice spread.

In 1921, Anoka, Minnesota, celebrated the first official city-wide Halloween with carved pumpkins, a costumed square dance, and two parades. After that, it didn't take Halloween long to go nationwide. New York started observing Halloween in 1923 and Los Angeles in 1925.

Sharpen your pun cells now, and please join us for some punnery about our favorite Halloween creatures—vampires, ghosts, skeletons, witches, and other monsters.

A Feast of Halloween Foods

What do you call an empty hot dog? Answer: A hollow weenie.

Here's a menu of more Halloween treats for the holiday: We know you won't be able to resist goblin up this full-corpse meal. Bone appétit!

Grains

Ghost Toasties   Scream of Wheat

Pentagram Crackers with Poisonbury Jam

Brain Muffins

Entrees

Hungarian Ghoul Ash   Frank 'n' Stein

Stake Sandwitch with Grave-y   Holloweenie

Cape-on   Blood Pudding

Littleneck Clams   Black Catfish

Bagels with Warlocks and Scream Cheese

Side Dishes

Deviled Eggs	Strangled Eggs
Artery-chokes	Skullions
Scarrots	Ghost Liver Pâté
Pickled Bats	Spook-ghetti
Gangreens	Baked Bones

Fruits

Adam's Apples	Necktarines

Desserts

Eye Scream	Boobury Pie
Boo Meringue	Ghoul Whip
Terrormisu	Ladyfingers
Ghoulda Cheese	Monster Cheese

Creep Suzette

Beverages

Ghoul Ade	Coffin with Scream
Apple Spider	Bloody Mary

What do you get when you drop a pumpkin?

Squash.

What's the favorite food of mathematicians?

Pumpkin pi.

What do you call a yokel living on a farm at Halloween?

A country pumpkin.

How do predatory canines find their way around at night?

They carry jackal lanterns.

Baby ghosts are often sent to dayscare centers and noisery schools and are advised: "Don't spook until you're spooken to." Their mothers also tell them, "Put your boos and shocks on" and "Don't forget to boo-ckle your sheet belt" and remind them to say, "How do you boo, sir or madam?"

What's a ghost's favorite breakfast cereal? Ghost Toasties.

favorite children's games: hide and shriek and peek-a-boo!

favorite children's toy: a haunted doll house.

favorite amusement rides: the scare-ousel and the roller ghoster.

favorite mode of transportation: scareplane.

favorite places to shop: boo-tiques.

favorite street: a dead end.

favorite fictional detective: Sherlock Moans.

Now that the ghost is clear, it's time for some spirited puns about ghosts and skeletons. You have more than a ghost of a chance of avoiding boo-boos and coming up the right answers.

How does an exorcist keep in shape?

He rides an exorcycle.

What happens when you fire your exorcist?
You get ex-spelled and repossessed.

What do you call a chicken that haunts your house?
The poultrygeist.

What kind of songs to ghosts prefer?
Haunting melodies.

What do you get when you cross Bambi with a ghost?
Bamboo.

What do you call a ghost who haunts small hotels?
An inn specter.

Why did the game warden arrest the ghost?
He didn't have a haunting license.

Why does an elevator makes ghosts happy?
Because it lifts the spirits.

What do you call a ghostbuster?
A spooksperson.

What helps ghostly musicians to play melodies?
Sheet music.

What do spooks call their navy?
The Ghost Guard.

Where do ghosts learn to become pilots?
At fright school.

What do you call the ghosts of dead turkeys?
Gobblins.

Where do cowboy goblins live?
In ghost towns.

What happens when a ghost haunts a theater?
The actors get stage fright.

Unfortunately, not a single skeleton attended the Halloween banquet. They had no body to go with, they didn't have the stomach for it, and they had no guts.

Now, are you ready to bone up on skeleton jokes? We're sure that they'll tickle your funny bone:

What's a skeleton's favorite food? Spare ribs.

favorite place to eat: the cadaver-teria.

favorite historical figure: Napoleon Bone-apart.

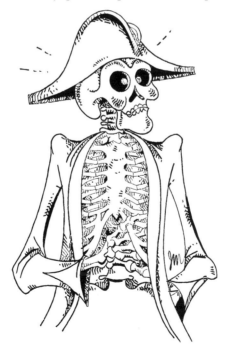

favorite fictional detective: Sherlock Bones.

best subject in school: Anatomy.

favorite vacation retreat: Maliboo.

What do you call a skeleton who goes outside in winter with no hat on?

> *A numb skull.*

What's the scariest job in the world?

> *The graveyard shift with a skeleton crew.*

What do you call a skeleton who won't get out of bed?

> *Lazy bones.*

Why aren't there any famous skeletons?

> *They're a bunch of no bodies.*

How do you deliver mail to skeletons?

> *By bony express.*

And as skeletons say to their friends who are going on cruises, "Bone voyage!"

Witchful Thinking

Halloween is also the time for witchful thinking. Witches are flying sorcerers who operate a fly-by-night operation. On Halloween, they swoop through the air like scareplanes, and we're here to share the black magic jokes about them.

To make themselves attractive, witches go to the boo-ty parlor to purchase some scare spray and mass-scare-a. Then they hop on their brooms and sweep through the Halloween skies. They avoid riding their brooms when they're angry because they tend to fly off the handle. If their broom happens to break, they witch-hike or they call broom service.

A little-known fact is that witches themselves actually go trick-or-treating and collecting goodies in their Wicca baskets. One witch draped herself with several strings of blinking Christmas-tree bulbs. She was a lights witch.

What was the witch's favorite subject in school?

Spelling.

When the witch said, "Abracadabra," nothing happened. She was a hopeless speller.

One witch told another witch, "I want one of those new computers that has a spell checker."

Why did the witches have to cancel their baseball game?

Their bats flew away.

What do you call a witch who lives at the beach?

A sand witch.

What do you call a snake that keeps witches away from their parked cars?

A witch shield viper.

How do witches tell time?

On their witch watches.

Have you heard about the witch who contracted a skin disease from her pet?

She went from bat to warts.

Who is the most famous witch detective?

Warlock Holmes.

Word Prey in a Jugular Vein

Vampires love to drink blood because they find it thicker than water. In fact, we know a vampire who was fired as night watchman at a blood bank. They caught him drinking on the job, thus making too many unauthorized withdrawals. And he took too many coffin breaks.

Long ago vampires sailed to the United States in blood vessels and set up their own terror-tories. Some settled in the Vampire State, and others went west and became batboys for the Colorado Rockies' Horror Picture Show. Some went on to college and earned a place in Phi Batta Cape-a.

Vampires from all over the world gather each fall in Transylvania to renew their commitment to their calling. They reverently view the scroll, written and signed in blood, that contains their history and lists their rites and responsibilities. Then, at midnight, they stand at attention and swear allegiance to the Draculation of Vein Dependence.

Vampire parents tell their vampire children at an early age, "Whatever else you do, NEVER run with a wooden stake in your hands. Remember, your life's at stake." Also: "Eat your meal before it clots" and "Always bite the hand that feeds you." Even with this sound advice, vampire children can become spoiled bats and drive their parents batty.

The most famous of all vampires is, of course, Count Dracula, the notorious neck romancer. He can be a real pain in the neck, but he can get under your skin. Even if he pays for dinner, he'll still put the bite on you.

Dracula once fell in love at first fright with the girl necks door. She was six feet tall, and Dracula loves to suck up to women. But he's remained a bat-chelor his whole life because anytime he courts another vampire, they end up at each other's throats.

And any mortal woman Dracula is attracted to soon realizes that life with him will be an unfailingly draining experience, so she's not likely to stick her neck out for him. It's hard to get a good night's sleep with him because of the terrible coffin.

Moreover, Dracula isn't a very attractive fellow, in large part because he can't see himself in the bat room mirror and so is unable to brush his teeth, comb his hair, or tie his tie. This causes bat breath and the disease Dracula fears most—tooth decay. The fiend went to the dentist to correct his bite, but he still ended up with false teeth, which for him are new-fangled devices that, like Dracula himself, come out at night.

Dracula finds his victims in any neck of the woods. Whenever the police come after him, the count simply explains that he is a law-a-biting citizen. He hopes that his victims won't cross him and that the cops won't have a stakeout.

Dracula loves the deep plots and grave setting of a cemetery, especially when the temperature rises above 90 degrees. The Count often sighs, "There's nothing like a cold bier on a hot day." Sometimes Dracula has to wait ages to emerge from his coffin. To him it seems that the sun never sets on the brutish vampire.

Among Dracula's favorite songs are "You're So Vein" and "I Left Her Heart in San Francisco."

his favorite TV show: "Nip at Night."

favorite comic-book character: Batman.

favorite candy: all-day sucker.

favorite magazine: "Bleeders Digest." (It has great circulation.)

favorite products: blood cell phones and #60 sun block.

favorite brand of facial tissue: Kleen-necks.

favorite dog: a bloodhound.

favorite cars: the bloodmobile and the Batmobile (especially for speeding along a major artery).

favorite sports: batminton and casketball.

least favorite word game: crosswords.

least favorite card game: high-stakes poker.

least favorite charity: the Red Cross.

favorite circus act: the jugulars.

favorite bodies of water: Lake Erie and the Dead Sea.

favorite holiday: Fangsgiving.

favorite dance: the fangdango.

Here are some puns that you can really sink your teeth into:

Did you hear about the vampire poet?

He went from bat to verse.

What did the vampire do when he saw a funeral procession?

He took a turn for the hearse.

What do vampires take for a sore throat?

Coffin drops.

Did you hear about the vampire's arithmetic homework assignment?

It was a blood count.

What's the difference between an optimist and a vampire killer?

One counts his blessings, and the other blesses his counts.

Why was the vampire expelled from school?

For failing the blood test.

Where do they keep imprisoned vampires?

In blood cells.

Who went to the vampires' family reunion?

All the blood relations.

Who does Dracula get letters from?

His fang club.

How can you spot a vampire jockey?

He always wins by a neck.

Vampire teacher: "How do you spell *coffin*?"

Little Dracula: "K-A-U-G-H-E-N."

Vampire teacher: "That's the worst coffin spell I have ever heard."

Did you hear about the unsuccessful vampire hunter?

He tried to kill a vampire by driving a pork chop through its heart because steaks were too expensive.

Knock, knock.

Who's there?

Ivan.

Ivan who?

Ivan to drink your blood.

Or, as Dracula said to his apprentice, "We could do with some new blood around here."

How did the race between two vampires end?

They finished neck and neck.

What is the motto of the vampire baby boom generation?

There's a sucker born every minute.

Why did the vampire wrestler get so many compound fractures?

Because people never give a sucker an even break.

Why did the vampire go into a fast-food restaurant?

For a quick bite.

How many vampires does it take to change a light bulb?

None. Vampires prefer the dark.

Vampires don't like to be crossed, but they often are, as the following curious clonings will show:

What do you get if you cross a vampire and a vegetarian?

Someone who tries to get blood from a turnip.

What do you get when you cross a snowman with a vampire?

Frostbite.

What do you get when you cross Dracula and a dog?

Something whose bite is worse than his bark.

What do you get when you cross Dracula and a duck?

Count Drakeula.

What do you get when you cross a vampire with a large antlered animal?

Vamoose.

Now it's time to say good-bye to Dracula and his batty friends: "So long, suckers!"

A Monstrous Halloween

Halloween is a time when we conjure up visions of all manner of ghoulies and ghosties and long-leggety beasties. Along with Dracula, the most popular of these creatures is the Frankenstein monster, not to be confused with Victor Frankenstein, his creator.

Despite his evil reputation, Dr. Victor Frankenstein actually had a good sense of humor; he kept his monster in stitches. Frankenstein was also a philanthropist because he founded the first organ donor program—a dead giveaway to his good heart. He also loved his dog—a black Lab, of course. And when the monster rose from the table and spat on the ground, the proud doctor exclaimed, "It's saliva! It's saliva!"

Even though Frankenstein's monster's twisted body strikes us as shocking and re-volting, he had his heart in the right place. In fact, he once had a ghoul friend to take out for a frank 'n' stein. He just couldn't resistor. He'd previously dated a lady scarecrow but went from rags to witches.

Sensitive fellow that old Zipperneck was, he also developed an identity crisis. He kept hoping that he had a mummy and dead-y, but they never appeared. So he went to a psychiatrist to see if he had a screw loose. One day he decided to take the five o'clock train. But the authorities made him give it back. Actually, the townspeople came to love Frankenstein's monster; to a man, they carried a torch for him.

Also prominent in our popular culture is the image of the werewolf. Did you know that werewolves love to eat sheep because they can dine and floss at the same time?

One day a fellow went to a clinic and complained, "Doctor, doctor! I feel like I'm a werewolf." The doctor replied, "Have a seat and comb your face."

Wolfman lived in San Francisco. When he felt mischievous, he would moon at the bay. Afterwards, he moved to Howlywood, where he auditioned for bit parts.

His lupine body caused him to get dirt on his clothes frequently, so he had to visit the Laundromat almost every day. He became a washin' werewolf. He also took up clay-spinning as a hobby and became a hairy potter.

Also enshrined in the Monsters Hall of Fame is the Invisible Man. Don't bother inviting the Invisible Man to your Halloween party. He won't show up. Sometimes he makes excuses, but they're all transparent. He isn't much to look at, and you can see right through them.

Invisible's mother and father were also invisible. They were trans-parents. When he was a teenager, he seldom hung out with his friends. Whenever he tried to make a point with his friends, they just said, "I don't see where you're coming from."

Recently, a number of movies featuring the Mummy have drawn big audiences who watch the action in Horrorscope. Off the silver screen the Mummy isn't very popular with the other monsters. They think he's egotistical because he's all wrapped up in himself. Being interested in band ages, he loves music, his favorite style being wrap!

As the sign in the Egyptian funeral home reads: "Satisfaction guaranteed or your mummy back!"

Why do you always find ghouls and demons together?
Because demons are a ghoul's best friend.

What did the ghoul buy for his ghoulfiend?
A set of his and hearse pajamas.

What did the ghoul shout when the diggers wanted to use his gravesite?
"You'll do it over my dead body!"

Where do ghouls get their mail?
At the dead-letter office.

How do ghouls and zombies begin their letters?

"Tomb it may concern."

Why do zombies play cards in a cemetery?

Just in case they have to dig up another player.

What is the favorite brand of toothpaste for little devils?

Imp-U-Dent.

What did the dead Superman say to the dead Lois Lane?

"Shall we sleep in the Kryptonite?"

Knock knock.

Who's there?

Zombies.

Zombies who?

Zombies make honey and zombies don't.

What do monsters say when something is really neat?

"Ghoul!"

Did you hear about the seriously ill zombie?

He's in grave condition.

Why was the zombie kicked out of the gravediggers' glee club?

Because he couldn't carry a tomb.

How do the corpses in graveyards send messages to each other?

Crypt-o-grams.

What happened to the monster children who ate all their vegetables?

They gruesome.

Who did the zombie invite to his party?

Anybody he could dig up.

Why did the doctor tell the zombie to get some rest?

He was dead on his feet.

What do you get if you cross a Scottish locksmith, a bird, and Frankenstein?

A lock nest monster.

Is it okay for a zombie to eat fried chicken with his fingers?

No, the fingers should be eaten separately.

Why did the monster eat a light bulb?

He was in need of a light snack, and it really made his eyes light up.

What did the evil chicken lay?

Deviled eggs.

Thanksgiving

*T*hanksgiving Day is mainly a celebration of the harvest, giving thanks for bountiful crops. Traditionally, a particular meal in 1621 is thought to be the first Thanksgiving. Plymouth colonists and Wampanoag Indians sat down together to an autumn feast of venison and wild fowl. This meal is remembered as a celebration not only of the harvest, but of the friendship and cooperation between the natives and the settlers.

On November 26, 1789, George Washington established the first national celebration of Thanksgiving. In 1863,

Abraham Lincoln, hoping to unite a sundered nation, issued a proclamation declaring Thanksgiving to be a national holiday to be celebrated on the last Thursday of November. Congress passed a joint resolution in 1941 decreeing that Thanksgiving should fall on the fourth Thursday of each November, where it remains. Harry S. Truman established the tradition of granting a presidential pardon to a Thanksgiving turkey, who is then retired, alive and gobbling, to a petting farm.

Food and family are the cornerstones of the holiday and are what we should be most thankful for in our lives. Thanksgiving traditions include preparing sumptuous meals that often include turkey, stuffing, gravy, sweet potatoes, cranberry sauce, and pumpkin pie.

Many of us decorate our homes with traditional signs of fall, such as the cornucopia, gourds, and autumn leaves. The cornucopia, or horn of plenty, is a representation of a hollow goat's horn, overflowing with fruit and other produce.

Around 88 percent of Americans eat turkey at Thanksgiving, consuming about 46 million birds. Three million people attend the Macy's Thanksgiving Day Parade annually, and 44 million watch it on TV.

How do Halloween and Thanksgiving differ?
One has goblins, and the other has gobblers.

If April showers bring May flowers, what do May flowers bring?
Pilgrims.

How did the Mayflower show that it liked America?
It hugged the shore,

If the Pilgrims came over on the Mayflower, how did the barbers arrive?
On clipper ships.

What kind of car did Pilgrims drive?
A Plymouth.

What kind of music would a Pilgrim like today?
Plymouth rock.

Why did the Pilgrims' pants always fall down?
Because they wore their buckles on their hats.

How are Puritans and small investors alike?
They have both been punished in stocks.

What's black and white and red all over?
A Pilgrim with a rash.

Why did the Indian chief wear so many feathers?
To keep his "wigwam."

What can you never eat for Thanksgiving dinner?
Breakfast or lunch.

What would Thanksgiving be like if the Pilgrims had landed in Africa instead of America?

We don't know, but we'd sure hate to have to stuff a hippopotamus.

I have some relatives with Mohawk haircuts, multiple facial piercings, and a lot of tattoos. What should I serve them at Thanksgiving?

Punk kin pie.

Are you serving a sweet potato casserole this year?

I yam.

Why should you keep your eye off the turkey dressing?

Because it makes him blush.

Why do turkeys hate Thanksgiving?

Because they're cut to pieces, they have the stuffing knocked out of them, and they're picked on for days after Thanksgiving.

What did the turkey say to the turkey hunter?

"Quack! Quack!"

Why did the musicians let the turkey join the band?

Because he had the drumsticks.

Why did the turkey cross the road?

It was the chicken's day off.

Why did the police arrest the turkey?

They suspected it of fowl play.

Why did the band leader save the drumsticks from 38 turkeys?

Because he wanted to play "76 tom bones."

Which side of the turkey has the most feathers?

The outside.

What's the best dance to do on Thanksgiving?

The turkey trot.

Why is a Thanksgiving turkey a fashionable bird?

Because he always appears well dressed for dinner.

What's a turkey's favorite song?

"I'm Dreaming of a White Christmas."

What key has legs and can't open doors?

A turkey.

What is the best thing to put into a turkey?

Your teeth.

What do you get when you cross a turkey with an octopus?

Enough drumsticks for a large Thanksgiving dinner.

What do you get when you cross a turkey with a banjo?

A turkey that can pluck itself.

What disasters could happen if you dropped the Thanksgiving turkey?

The downfall of Turkey, the breakup of China, and the overthrow of Greece.

What did the turkey say before it was roasted?

"I'm stuffed!"

What did the mother turkey say to her daughter as she ate?

"Don't gobble your food."

How do you make a turkey float?

You need two scoops of ice cream, some root beer, and a turkey.

What sort of glass would you serve cream of turkey soup in?

A goblet.

A Thanksgiving Weather Forecast

Turkeys will thaw in the morning, then warm in the oven to an afternoon high near 190°F. The kitchen will turn hot and humid, and if you bother the cook, be ready for a severe squall or cold shoulder.

During the late afternoon and evening, the cold front of a knife will slice through the turkey, causing an accumulation of one to two inches on plates. Mashed potatoes will drift across one side, while cranberry sauce creates slippery spots on the other. Please pass the gravy.

A weight watch and indigestion warning have been issued for the entire area, with increased stuffiness around the beltway.

During the evening, the turkey will diminish and taper off to leftovers, dropping to a low of 34°F in the refrigerator.

Looking ahead to Friday and Saturday, high pressure to eat sandwiches will be established. Flurries of leftovers can be expected both days with a 50 percent chance of scattered soup late in the week. We expect a warming trend where soup develops.

By early next week, eating pressure will be low, and the only wish left will be the bone.

Pop Goes the Turkey

The turkey shot out of the oven
And rocketed into the air.
It knocked every plate off the table
And partly demolished a chair.

It ricocheted into a corner
And burst with a deafening boom.
Then it splattered all over the kitchen,
Completely obscuring the room.

It stuck to the walls and the windows.
It totally coated the floor.
There was turkey attached to the ceiling
Where there'd never been turkey before.

It blanketed every appliance.
It smeared every saucer and bowl.
There wasn't a way I could stop it.
That turkey was out of control!

I scraped and I scrubbed with displeasure,
And thought with disgust as I mopped
That I'd never again stuff a turkey
With popcorn that hadn't been popped.

Chanukah

*C*hanukah (or Hanukkah) celebrates the first victory for religious freedom in history. Chanukah, the Jewish "Festival of Lights," lasts eight days and nights. Beginning on the 25th day of Kislev, the ninth month of the Jewish calendar, Chanukah typically occurs during late November or early December.

In the mid-second century B.C., the Syrians captured control of the Jewish Holy Temple in Jerusalem and rededicated it to their god Zeus. While this deeply wounded the Jewish people, they did not fight back against their more powerful opponents until King Antiochus the Great outlawed Judaism and decreed that all Jews were to worship Greek gods. This inspired an uprising known as the Maccabean Revolt, during which the Jews eventually ousted their Syrian oppressors and regained control of their holy place.

To purify the temple, which had been defiled by the conquerors, the Jews used a menorah, a type of oil-burning ritual candelabra, for the prescribed period of eight days. But they found that there was only about one day's worth of oil remaining in the temple. When they decided to burn the oil anyway, it miraculously lasted the whole eight days, giving birth to the annual ritual that is still observed today.

One small candle can create so much light.

The lighting of the Hanukkah candles is the central ritual of Chanukah, during which an eight-candled menorah is used. Each evening, one candle is kindled, accompanied by prayers, with an additional candle being lit on subsequent nights of the observance.

Games and gifts are also associated with Chanukah. The best-known of these games involves the dreidel, which is a four-sided top that children play with before or after the candle-lighting observance.

Top Ten Reasons Why Everyone Should Celebrate Chanukah

10. No big, fat guy getting stuck in your chimney.

9. No roof damage from reindeer hooves and their droppings.

8. Cleaning wax off your menorah is way easier than dismantling an eight-foot-tall fir tree.

7. Compare: chocolate gelt (coins) to fruitcake

6. If people mess up their gift, there are seven more days to correct it.

5. No brutal letdown when you discover that Santa Claus isn't real.

4. Your neighbors are unlikely to complain about how your menorah is blinding them.

3. It's like a big reunion when everyone gathers at the Chinese restaurant on Christmas Eve.

2. You can use your fireplace.

And the number-one reason why everyone should celebrate Chanukah is:

1. None of that naughty-or-nice stuff. Everyone gets loot.

The Eight Nights of Chanukah

On the first night of Chanukah, someone sent to me
A warm bagel topped with cream cheese.

On the second night of Chanukah, someone sent to me
Two matzo balls—
And a warm bagel topped with cream cheese.

On the third night of Chanukah, someone sent to me
Three golden latkes,
Two matzo balls—
And a warm bagel topped with cream cheese.

On the fourth night of Chanukah, someone sent to me
Four pounds of corned beef,
Three golden latkes,
Two matzo balls—
And a warm bagel topped with cream cheese.

On the fifth night of Chanukah, someone sent to me
Five kosher dills,
Four pounds of corned beef,
Three golden latkes,
Two matzo balls—
And a warm bagel topped with cream cheese.

On the sixth night of Chanukah, someone sent to me
Six grandmas cooking,
Five kosher dills,
Four pounds of corned beef,
Three golden latkes,
Two matzo balls—
And a warm bagel topped with cream cheese.

On the seventh night of Chanukah, someone sent to me
Seven rabbis dancing,
Six grandmas cooking,
Five kosher dills,
Four pounds of corned beef,
Three golden latkes,
Two matzo balls—
And a warm bagel topped with cream cheese.

On the eighth night of Chanukah, someone sent to me
Eight fiddlers fiddling,
Seven rabbis dancing,
Six grandmas cooking,
Five kosher dills,
Four pounds of corned beef,
Three golden latkes,
Two matzo balls—
And a warm bagel topped with cream cheese.

Christmas Eve / Christmas Day

C hristmas ("the mass of Christ") is a major global holiday. The Christmas story centers on the birth in Bethlehem of Jesus Christ of Nazareth. This took place in a stable because there was no room at the inn for Joseph, the Virgin Mary, and their newborn son.

Christmas Eve comes on December 24, followed by Christmas Day on December 25, a federal holiday since 1870. The holiday is a joyous occasion illuminated by candles, decorations, Christmas trees, poinsettias, traditional songs and carols, family feasts and parties, and the exchange of presents and greeting cards.

The modern Christmas lore of Santa Claus visiting homes around the world to leave gifts for children is rooted in the legend of Sinter Klaas. Dutch settlers brought that legend and lore to the New World during the 17th century. The Christmas traditions of trimming ornamental trees and hanging wreaths of holly and red, green, and silver decorations have become ingrained in Western culture. As with Chanukah, human beings yearn for stories of light shining down on them during the dead of winter, the darkest time of the year.

A Visit with St. Nicholas

On Christmas Eve, Santa Claus eats a jolly roll, leaps into his sleigh, and urges his toys to hop in the sack. Santa's sleigh always comes out first because it starts in the Pole position. The sleigh also gets terrific mileage because it has long-distance runners on each side.

Santa especially loves all his reindeer because every buck is deer to him. He puts bells on all his reindeer because their horns don't work. On the way to delivering gifts, he stops his sleigh at the Deery Queen. For this the deer offer him their Santapplause and sing, "Freezer Jolly Good Fellow!"

When traveling in the sleigh in bad weather, Santa gets icicles in his beard. Real chin chillas, those. He sometimes removes all the bells from his sleigh and travels silently through the night. One day he hopes to win a No Bell Prize.

Santa often guides his sleigh to Cape Canaveral. We know this because A SANTA AT NASA is a palindrome, a statement that reads the same forwards and backwards.

What's red and white and black all over? Santa Claus sliding down a chimney. Coming down chimneys really soots him. But he actually has a fear of getting stuck. That fear is called Santa Claus-trophobia. Occasionally Santa falls down a chimney. Then he's Santa Klutz. When Santa Claus falls into a lit fireplace, he becomes Crisp Cringle. Since Santa has to go up and down a wide variety of chimneys on Christmas, he always gets a yearly flue shot.

Santa is so Santa-mental that he sometimes spends all his money on the toys that he brings to children everywhere. At those times, he's called St. Nickelless.

How do cats greet each other at Christmas?

"Have a Furry Meowy Christmas and a Happy Mew Year!"

How do sheep greet each other at Christmas?

"Season's Bleetings and Fleece Navidad! Fleece on earth, good wool to men!"

Punning is a rewording experience, especially around Christmas time. That's when people exchange hellos and good buys with each other, the time of year when every girl wants her past forgotten and her presents remembered, the time of year when mothers have to separate the men from the toys.

A Punderful Christmas Game

What's the difference between a one-winged angel and a two-winged angel?

It's a matter of a pinion.

It's a matter of our opinion that Yule love the game you're about to play. In each sentence below, fill in the blank or blanks with an expression commonly used at Christmastide or with an outrageous holiday pun. Answers appear right after the game, but don't sneak a peek until you've tried your hardest.

1. On December 24, Adam's wife was known as Christmas _____.

2. In Charles Dickens's *A Christmas Carol*, Scrooge was visited by the ghost of Christmas _____.

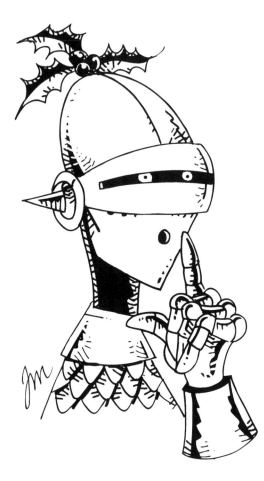

3. An opinion survey in Alaska is called a North _____.

4. What does Santa Claus do with his three gardens? _____, _____, _____!

5. What Christmas message is conveyed by these letters?

ABCDEFGHIJKMNOPQRSTUVWXYZ

ABCDEFGHIJKMNOPQRSTUVWXYZ. _____ _____, _____ _____.

6. What do you call an ephant and a cam at Christmas?

    _____ _____, _____ _____.

7. When the salt and the pepper say "Hi!" to each other, they are passing on _____ greetings.

8. If athletes get athlete's foot, then astronauts get _____

    _____.

9. When you cross a sheep with a cicada, you get a Baaa! _____!

10. A quiet medieval armor-wearer is a _____ Knight.

11. A cat walking on the desert is bound to get Sandy_____.

12. A Christmas bird dog is a _____ _____.

Answers

1. Christmas Eve 2. Christmas Present 3. North Poll 4. Hoe, hoe, hoe! 5. Noel, Noel (no *l,* no *l*) 6. Noel, Noel (no *el,* no *el*)

7. seasons' greetings 8. missile toe 9. Baaa! Humbug! 10. Silent Knight 11. Sandy Claws 12. point setter

When does Christmas come before Thanksgiving?
In the dictionary.

What do you say to a bad puppy at Christmas?
"Felix, naughty dog!" (Feliz Navidad!)

What do you call a manufacturer of turkey filling?
A stuffing stocker.

What do you get when you cross Santa Claus with a tramp?
A ho-ho-hobo.

What do elves learn in school?

The elf-abet.

Why are Christmas trees like bad knitters?

They both drop their needles.

Why do movie stars burn in their fireplaces at Christmas time?

Holly wood.

What do you get when you cross a gift-wrapper with a wise guy?

Ribbon Hood.

Who hides in the bakery at Christmas?

A mince spy.

Have you heard that they're planning to combine Chanukah and Christmas?

The new song for the amalgamated holiday will be "Oy Vay, Maria."

Did you hear about the dyslexic devil worshipper?

He sold his soul to Santa.

What do you call a ghost hanging around Santa's Workshop?

A North Pole-tergeist.

What happened to the little boy who swallowed Christmas tree trimmings?

He experienced tinselitis.

Why did the little girl say when she was invited to portray the Virgin in a Christmas pageant?

"Oh, good. Now I can eat, drink, and be Mary."

On Christmas eve, a burglar broke into the home of a lawyer. The thief took all the lawyer's Christmas gifts from under the tree but left the packages for the wife and children alone.

As the criminal was leaving the house, he was caught by a policeman. He confessed to what he did but told the policeman that he couldn't be arrested. The policeman asked why, and the thief responded, "Because the law states that I'm entitled to the presents of an attorney."

Knock knock.

Who's there?

Santa.

Santa who?

Santa package by FedEx, so it should arrive by Christmas.

Knock knock.

Who's there?

Centipede.

Centipede who?

Centipede on the Christmas tree.

Knock knock.
Who's there?
Donut.
Donut who?
Donut open till Christmas.

Knock knock.
Who's there?
Dexter.
Dexter who?
Dexter halls with boughs of holly.

Knock knock.
Who's there?
Avery.
Avery who?
Avery merry Christmas to you!

Merry Christmas to all! And remember: There's No Plate Like Chrome for the Hollandaise.

Rudolph's Day

Christmas was over. Santa Claus and his reindeer finally had a chance to rest. They had done a good job, and they deserved it.

Rudolph the Red-Nosed Reindeer had a chance to do something he had wanted to do for a long time. He made an appointment with a plastic surgeon because he was so sensitive about his looks. It wasn't his glowing red nose that he wanted changed. He was proud of that nose and the help he and it had given to Santa. No, he was sensitive about his long ears, which were much bigger than the ears of the average reindeer, or rabbit for that matter.

So one week after Christmas, Rudolph's doctor performed the surgery, and since that time, January 1 has been known as New Ears Day.

Also Available: